S0-CID-407

Indeterminate Inflorescence

LEE SEONG-BOK

Indeterminate Inflorescence

Lectures on Poetics

Translated from the Korean
by Anton Hur

an object by
SUBLUNARY EDITIONS
of Seattle, WA

무한화서
© 2015 Lee Seong-bok
First published in Korea in 2015 by Moonji Publishing Co, Ltd.
All rights reserved.

Translation © 2023 Anton Hur

ISBN 978-1-955190-62-6

All rights reserved. Except for brief passages quoted in a review,
regardless of medium, no part of this book may be reproduced in
any form or by any means, electronic or mechanical, including
photocopying and recording, or by any information storage and re-
trieval system, without permission in writing from the Publisher.

Wholesale available at asterismbooks.com

Design and typesetting by Joshua Rothes.
Cover photo by Joshua Rothes; handwritten text by Rebecca Coster.

Typeset in Linotype Sabon Next and Din Pro,
with Korean characters set in Malgun Gothic

CONTENTS

INDETERMINATE INFLORESCENCE

LANGUAGE

○.

"Inflorescence" is the order in which flowers bloom on a stem. An alternative word for inflorescence in "pure Korean" is "flower-sequence" (kkotcharae). There are two kinds of inflorescence: "Determinate inflorescence" means flowers bloom from top to bottom (basipetal) with limited growth. "Indeterminate inflorescence" means the flowers bloom from bottom to top (acropetal), and growth is un-limited. We might say poems bloom in "indeterminate inflorescence" as they grow from concrete to abstract, from secular to sacred.

Poetry takes its form in its endless failure to express what language cannot.

I.

Poetry is what is unsayable. To blurt out what is unsayable is to ignore this fundamental premise.

2.

Poetry is an encounter with unexpected truth. What awaits us when we begin writing a poem is the unknown; only the unwritten can make us happy. Poetry is the promise of joy in the as-yet unknown.

3.

Language can be messy or vulgar, yet without it there is no seeing or hearing. Language is not a means to an end but an object and objective in itself. To use it as a mere tool only leads to unhappiness. Writing is language in the act of escaping and adventuring into the unknown.

4.

When writing poetry, the words must always be separated from the self. Otherwise, the words become oppressed by the brain.

5.

Unlike theorists, writers are completely dependent on the compulsion of language. It's language that casts the net. Writers haul it in. Once you grasp this, you'll never have to rely on theories again.

6.

That a wealth of experience is essential to write poetry is a myth rooted in the mistaken belief that poetry exists within the poet. Neither is poetry in objects. When Wang Shouren tried to achieve a wider understanding of things through the investigation into the essence of bamboo, his efforts only left him heartsick. Poetry ultimately resides in language; thus language, corrupted as it is by the real world, is sacred. Poets and objects may be nothing more than the hosts poems pass through before sprouting the wings of language.

7.

At one end of the poetic spectrum is beauty and abstraction; at the other, truth and concreteness. To focus on beauty dilutes truth, leaving only pure music, an expression of taste. This is audible poetry, which moves from the present to the future. To focus on truth exposes what's hidden, and meaning sharpens into view. This is visible poetry, which moves from the present to the past. Poetry exists between these two extremes.

8.

In Seon Buddhism, "to see what's fundamental" is understood as "to see is fundamental". Perhaps poems can arise from switching subject and verb, what is seeing and what is seen.

9.

One and only one image can carry over many emotions; no emotion can carry over one and only one image.

10.

We do not give voice to our poems when we write them; our poems, rather, give voice to us. Words, in a sense, give voice to themselves through us. Perhaps that's the meaning of the phrase *veritas veritatum* (truth begets truth).

11.

The self can never speak itself; the speaking self would be left behind. If that speaking self speaks the self again, *that* speaking self would be left behind. Poetry takes its form in its endless failure to speak what cannot be spoken.

12.

To write poetry is to dig a waterway for words. Poetry allows words to flow through you. The poet must not force the flow of words but rather watch and wait.

13.

To write poetry is to create a way for words to pass. The poet must not drag words through you but rather watch them flow through you.

14.

Literature isn't made by us. Literature is made by language. There is no path that language cannot enter. Language can't even be talked about without language.

15.

The only thing that can be depended upon is language. But sharing a father doesn't mean we're all siblings. When our languages are different, we might as well be cats and dogs to each other.

16.

We distrust language even as we write poetry. We treat it like a lazy servant. But language is greater than us. You have to believe in language to be guided by it.

17.

Weak poems are weak because language was not treated with proper reverence. Language is the alpha and omega of poetry. But just because language is the only true refuge, it doesn't mean it has to take the forms of poetry.

18.

Our world is a world made of language. If you go "beyond language," there is only more language, and even these very words are language. A poet is someone who makes naked contact with this language.

19.

You must pluck the poem from yourself as quickly as possible. If you're thinking about the poem, it's already too late. Make sure you expel the words faster than you can think about them. Don't let your brain interfere. The stronger the poem's rhythm, the weaker its "meaning." A good sign that your brain is going faster than your body.

20.

The brain is deliberate and social, but the hand is closer to desire and the unconscious. A poem is like a finger that breaks out of your head. Or the slit in a Chinese qipao dress: opens when you walk, closes when you stop.

21.

Words dragged by force from the brain are stiff and devoid of feeling. Instead, your words should be a beat ahead of your brain. Like a child rolling a steel hoop, the words will come alive only if they roll on ahead of the brain.

22.

You've seen soccer players pass the ball to each other. If they're blocked, they pass, and receive the ball again once they're past the block. Just like this, you've got to let go of the language before thinking about what to do next. If you keep the ball in your possession, the reader will only steal it from you.

23.

The theme comes after the words. Don't write on a theme, write with words. It's difficult to build on meaning. Meaning arrives only after sound does.

24.

You know the feeling of stroking your beard against the grain? If the words are as weak as that friction, it becomes prose. Poetry on the other hand must make people feel unsettled, nothing more, nothing less.

25.

Poems written with intent is violence against poetry. You need to rescue language from the brain and make it dance in your body instead. Then both you and language will be happy.

26.

Poetry is the dance of words. The joy of poetry comes from the friction and tactile differences between words. There needs to be an eroticism above all. Words have a kind of instinct for going in and out. Have sex with words. So that new words are born beyond the current horizon of words.

27.

Write as if you've opened yourself in front of words and are asking them questions. Putting words first makes emotions follow, but putting emotions first makes even the emotions flee.

28.

You can't perfectly reproduce the feeling of the old who are sick and unconscious. Or of children who are running a high fever. But writing is still better at that than any camera or camcorder. That's why language is so precious.

29.

Our brain capacity is about that of a personal computer. Writing is like connecting this computer to a central processing node. Writing allows us to use the infinite information of the Internet that is language.

30.

This is an anecdote from a film titled *The Long Ships*. People searching for a golden bell by digging all over an island eventually give up and throw down their hoes. As the hoes strike the ground, they hear the sound of a bell. The entire island has been a bell this whole time. The moment their hoes become useless, the tools are reborn as musical instruments. Language, when used in poetry, is something like this.

31.

The first line of a poem is like the trigger of a gun. The next line follows it automatically, and the next after that. You do not speak words, instead you listen to the sound words make. Words and lines, like beasts, have mouths and tails. Each word or line has its tail in the mouth of the next one that follows it out into the world.

32.

A ripe watermelon will split open at the slightest graze of a knife. You are the one taking out the first words in a poem, but words are really what splits the poem open into life. We can move up from dimension to dimension thanks to words. Don't forget that each dimension is the shadow of the dimension above it.

33.

The rhythm of poetry is like that of a mourner's. Two steps forward, one step back... the fluttering funereal banners and the colorful paper flowers... listening to the sad singing and the sound of ghosts.

34.

Reality and rhythm are alive in colloquial language. Images as well, like the speck of rice germ on a grain of rice. For example, you can be made aware of how vividly alive rhythm and images are when listening to someone cursing their head off.

35.

Your words must be small and tread lightly. The lightness of "may" is more powerful than "shall". They say that Mencius, with his preference for the decisive postposition "ye (也)", was a second-rate sage to Confucius, who preferred the more ambivalent postposition "yi (矣)". Mencius's words, "Even a sage appearing three thousand years later shall not change what I say", (百世聖人復起不易吾言) lose strength under the weight of their arrogance.

36.

Poetry is where things miss the mark or go against the grain. Like linking "library" with "underwear" instead of "books".

37.

Just as parting is the moment of realizing the true depth of one's love, the importance of rhythm is felt only when the rhythm is broken.

38.

There are two kinds of sexual "deviance". One is that which deviates from the "purpose" of reproduction, and the other from the "object" of the opposite sex. The language of poetry is also perhaps seriously deviant in its abandoning of its purpose of conveying intent, and its object being that of expression not content, music not meaning.

39.

Always rely on the spoken word. It's precious because it's light and disappears easily. Like our lives...

40.

When writing poetry, you need to roll the words around your mouth like candy. Beethoven is said to have gotten the main theme for a quartet piece when he overheard a debtor shouting, "I don't have any money!"

41.

"Mug" is a more vibrant word than "face". Vernacular language is living language. Profanities and slang are poetic treasure chests.

42.

Write as closely to the vernacular as possible. That'll bring out the rhythm and style of your poems. You can tell from just its first line whether a poem was written with the brain or the mouth. Say the lines out loud, prod them with your tongue. The content doesn't matter at all. Or to be more accurate, only by writing with your mouth will your content shine.

43.

Writing relies on physical rhythms. Rhythm comes first, and you just have to ride it. Stop thinking and jump on. You only need one foot on the escalator to start going up. Or raise a hand at a truck to hitch a ride. You can always get off later. When prose rides rhythm it becomes poetry, and when poetry leaves rhythm it becomes prose. And translationese is the worst, ever.

44.

Writing poetry is easier if you imagine a conversation partner. If you pretend your friend or spouse is sitting next to you, words will naturally come flowing out of your mouth.

45.

Don't be scared of poetry. Write as if you're whispering intimately to yourself or someone next to you. But remember: half of speaking is silence. Don't forget, also, that in order to say something, you have to say it through something else.

46.

When the poem refuses to come to life, change the way you speak. Naturalness comes before rhythm. Forcing the rhythm necessitates "dentures" down the road. Without "as it is"-ness, writing is like children mistakenly trying to stuff their heads through the sleeve of a jacket.

47.

No matter how sad the story, pain always decreases after having spoken it. No matter how hard physical labor can be, putting it to song lightens the burdens carried. It's because of rhythm. It's the rhythm of work and the rhythm of the body. Whereas if you warn yourself to be careful as you go down the stairs, your feet will trip. That's the type of chaos that happens when your brain interferes with your body. Have your body write your poems, not your brain.

48.

Writing poems with your brain is like putting on foundation without having cleansed first. When you write, just push into it without thinking. Thinking should come later. The saying, "Waiting will make tardiness, and thinking will make mistakes," is more apt for writing than any other kind of activity.

49.

Kick against words like you would kick back on a swing. You've got to feel as if the soles of your feet are touching the sky.

50.

Our hands always speak the truth. Trust your hands and write as fast as you can.

51.

Don't go for knockouts every single time. You've got to jab with your words for a bit. A desire to hit a homerun will only make you strike out. Much like you would slightly hold out a baseball bat, stick your tongue out and gently poke a word first.

52.

The things we're trying to say are not in our brains but in our words. Relax your shoulders and just say what's on your mind. Once you see a gap, go straight for the uppercut.

53.

Mount a poem lightly. Like it's a bike or a horse saddle, or a running tiger. You just have to get used to the rhythm from there on. There really isn't much else for you to do. Let the rhythm "permeate" into you.

54.

"The empress tree is blooming, it blooms without a drop of blood, it blooms without a single breath…" Draw the words out like you would draw out a chain. That's all there is to it.

55.

Keep rolling around words in your mouth like candy. Words that butt in, stick, and stain are the best ones.

56.

Keep rolling the words in your mouth to make other words stick to them. Language seems foolish and a mess, but the only way to escape language is through language. Always get ready to transfer onto a word going in the opposite direction. If you come by a pebble in the road, the first thing you should think of is whether you should change the pebble in your pocket for it.

57.

There's a line taught in Vipassana meditation: "Make a new mind, and make the new mind see the old mind." You've got to make the new image latch onto the old image. The same goes for word to word, line to line, and stanza to stanza.

58.

Don't write like a searchlight passing over a landscape.

Each word has to bring forth the next one until the whole landscape shows up. If the next word isn't connected to the one before, it might as well be the beginning of a new piece of writing. Don't try to be flashy, just write like you would eat an ordinary meal. Try not to infuse your writing with your emotions. That's like getting your spit on your cooking; it'll spoil the food.

59.

I say this often, but a poem is a collection of words that were trying to get away. When you're joining the next line to the previous one, the new line has to be the same as the old but different. You'll know what the last line is only when you get there. Like how you'll know how you die only when you die.

60.

The first step in writing a poem is drunkenness and mania, but the second step is like an algebraic formula. You've got to build up each line like bricks in a strong brick wall. Poetic solutions are much trickier than mathematical ones. Not only does each individual have a different experience of language, but language itself is such a mess of a melting pot.

61.

Because poetry must use language, which is inherently opaque and unstable, it has to be more precise than mathematics. For poets, there is no higher morality than precision.

62.

They say oil paintings need underpainting to create truly profound colors. Flashy words mean there is no substance to them. Your methods need to be hidden. Don't be all breathless and breezy, in other words.

63.

Don't get too caught up in the primary definition of a word. This isn't to say you should write vaguely. The vagueness of a poem refers to the vagueness of its meaning, not its grammatical vagueness.

64.

Grab a few details and herd the story into one direction. Like linking stars to create a constellation. Make the overall setting clear. Withdraw all fancy rhetoric. They're like "dead stones" on a Go board. Anything that sounds fancy is just bullshit. If you don't really feel it, don't go overboard with it. Because that's simply fraudulence.

65.

Poetry is like holding a short sword and running straight into the fray. It's a hundred-meter dash. What's there to ramble on about in that time? The less you say, the fewer mistakes you make.

66.

When a whale swims, it uses its fins to change direction and its trunk to propel itself forward. In poetry, metaphors are like fins. Use them only when you must. They shouldn't be used for going forward.

67.

When playing the zither, you must press down lightly if you want a deep and soft tone. This lightness is more important than decorating your poem with fancy images.

68.

Rock climbers run ropes through a peg, take a step up, and drive another peg into the rock face. Writing a poem is like throwing forth another word from the word you've previously written. Your life hangs in the balance, so you shouldn't just carelessly toss your words. You've got to throw just far enough for you to be able to reach.

69.

When nurses give you a shot, they don't just jab you anywhere. They find a vein and tap it first. It's the same when you begin writing a poem. You can't just end a poem, either. You have to cover it up, like sweeping your hands over the eyelids of a dead person. Like a certain African tribe that punctures the necks of cows and sucks the blood out with a straw before covering the wound with a cowpat.

70.

We wrap our glassware with old newspapers when we move houses. Writing poems is like that. If you don't handle your words carefully, they'll end up chipped.

71.

Just write down the thoughts in your head. Writing easily is the fastest way through. No need to write dramatic thoughts about the destiny of the human race. There are plenty of such poems already. Just write down how many spoons you have in your kitchen.

72.

Words that don't seem meaningful at first when you hear them but strangely bother you over dinner—these are your most powerful words. It is said when a person is fatally injured, they'll say, "I'm fine…" and die right away. The best words are those that don't make an impression in the beginning but later make you go, "Oh!"

73.

A title like "My Older Brother" is a good one. That's a sentence that carries around the weight of an entire life. Like a watery ditch in the middle of a road, all kinds of desperate lives have gathered inside it.

74.

Poetry is when a part shows the whole, and a poem is a whole that crumbles when you take off a part. Weigh each bit with emotion. Poetry is words that smear, words that stain the heart. There is only poetry and not-poetry. There's no such thing as something that is "like poetry".

75.

You've seen slow-motion videos of a boxer's face being crumpled by a punch. That's the best feeling. Or videos where a ball warps against a bat … If you can get your words to recreate that feeling, you can die and go to heaven right away.

76.

You get verbose when you're not saying what you really want to say. Erase all those words and make a new start from the point where you felt you've said everything.

77.

Poetry is not emotion or metaphor but patterns. Patterns are retrospective and predictive at the same time. There are no patterns without metaphoric meaning. Patterns both come from and enable metaphor.

78.

When writing poems, you must create patterns using the twisting and turning of words. Three or four twists are enough. More than that, and the brain won't follow. "The man is not not not unkind" makes you uncertain whether the man is kind or not.

79.

If you say everything you want to say at once, there's no opportunity for poetry to sneak in. Say it slant. Don't speak directly toward the listener but a little bit off to the side. No direct attacks; use guerilla warfare. They say that if you want to send your golf ball into the nine o'clock direction, you've got to hit it not from three o'clock but somewhere between four and five o'clock.

80.

A restauranteur thinks of not only the taste of his ingredients but their color. Color, apparently, affects taste.

Poetry is also a form of display. If you place words in unfamiliar positions, all sorts of weird things happen.

81.

Don't paint over or lacquer a painting that's finished. When one poetic meaning breaks down, it'll simply be replaced with another one in the same moment. All meaning comes and goes over a desert of meaninglessness, like some mirage. The virtue of poetry is in how it endures meaninglessness for as long as possible.

82.

The filament of a lightbulb is a site of resistance. Without this filament, the current will short. Similarly, poetry is the spark that occurs from the resistance of the words occurring when two things are linked together.

83.

Poetry is a high-voltage current. If there's no spark, that's not a poem. The spark that is poetry occurs between words and between lines. Write like a neon sign that's drab during the day but lights up brilliantly in the night.

84.

Poetry reflects and refracts language. Poetry writing makes you feel the fun in words. Try making twists and falls. If you keep at it, the likelihood of success will increase. As long as you don't give up, you will always be able to reach new heights, if not the very top.

85.

Poetry is the power of the twist. There has to be some transition between lines and stanzas. Connections like "The flowers bloomed / The birds died" are stronger than "The flowers bloomed / The birds sang."

86.

Try peeling back a word, like: "You can't spell 'funeral' without 'fun.'" A funeral is a "fun era" that's come to an end because of a coffin ("l"). If you keep peeling back words like onions, you'll be left with nothing. Poetry shows that there is nothing behind a sign.

87.

You have to be able to factorize anything. Just like green can be factorized into yellow and blue, the French word orange can be divided into *or* (gold) and *ange* (angel). Poetry is the explanation of how "gold" and "angel" met to create "orange."

88.

When you create a metaphor using *a* for *b*, you have to make sure you profit from using *a*. Otherwise, you're just treading water.

89.

Every metaphor has to reproduce meaning. Metaphors can't be afterthoughts. Don't use metaphors that are too flashy. Only the ability to speak of boring beauty will lead you into victory.

90.

When $a = b$, try bringing c instead of b to talk about a. Try substituting some of c's qualities with those of a's. It's like experimenting with how a germ changes depending on the presence of different germs. But if the poet does not have a point in mind, it's all just an exercise to kill time.

91.

Poetry is the replacing of worn-down joints by switching out suffixes, auxiliary verbs, and conjunctions. If you don't change them, the words will come out half-steamed. And rice that hasn't been well-steamed doesn't taste good.

92.

The slope of a poem is determined by conjunctions like "and" or "but". "And" is too slight and "but" is too steep. The right slope is, perhaps, "however". It's like the cog-wheel that helps the belt shift easily.

93.

When you're connecting words together, make your strides wide. If there's a problem, you can always go back later and fix it. You've got to give yourself leeway. Try to stride as widely as possible. There's more hope in wide, ambitious failure than narrow, safe success.

94.

Unlike asexual reproduction, where species do not change, sexual reproduction requires recombination and the endless evolution of the species. Write like you're reproducing sexually, not asexually. Try "the fires of the river" and not "the tears of the river." Asexual reproduction is the way to a dead sentence, and sexual reproduction is the way to a living one.

95.

"The sun is shining" is a dead sentence. "The sun is crying" is closer to a living one. Living sentences have teeth. Even between the lines. "The sun is crying. A familiar face."

96.

When you're writing a poem, it's hard to recapture that "form" in your mind once you've lost it. When you have it, you've got to make wide enough strides that will allow you to fill in any gaps later on. Which also means that at some point, you've got to go back and fill these gaps in; otherwise, you'll end up with Seon koans.

97.

Try riding the rhythm when you're writing, like riding a wave. Any part that's too off the mark, you can always cut away later. But the underlying rhythm or "form" in your expression has to be alive. This form creates a pleasing drop, that feeling of released window blinds falling into place. Energy comes from resistance.

98.

It's this "form" that creates poetry; metaphor isn't what creates poetry. Form that's revealed is superficial and ornamental. It's like dead branches on a living tree. You've got to quickly trim them off.

99.

Poetic language is as precise as a cheetah biting into an antelope's vulnerable spot. For the sake of that one moment, you've got to keep throwing forth words like a dog frantically licking a hot dish.

OBJECT

100.

The profane is the energy source of poetry. It's profitable
when traces of fear come off from daily mundanities.
Stories that seem just within our grasp but elude us in
the end. Positions of no hope or compensation, positions headed nowhere, the same position yesterday
and tomorrow!

101.

Metaphors are unnecessary in poetry. A poem is already a
metaphor in itself. Just like the whole island is made of
gold in the film Longships, our whole reality itself is poetry.

102.

Poetry isn't about putting together striking metaphors.
Kim Sowol's "Flowers on the Hills" doesn't contain a
single overt metaphor. Because he speaks of people when
he speaks of flowers, that in itself is a metaphor.

103.

Take incidents simply. That's how poems can be steeped
from them. Poetry is what rides incidents, the incident

itself isn't poetry. Instead of trying to make poetry out of an incident, try to make the incident a metaphor for life.

104.

When you write a poem, don't drag it from the front but push it from the back. It's this assuming of the passive position that's the hardest and most important issue at hand. Only the strongest poet has the ability to be passive.

105.

Present the situation simply, and let the situation itself speak. Let the situation reach the point where it betrays itself. Don't force it to, let the situation do the work. The situation knows a lot more than we do.

106.

When swinging a golf club, they say not to "surprise the ball". This means to not determinedly hit the ball in an attempt to send it far. Writing poetry is the same. Casually meet the object, and casually send it away.

107.

The best way is to imitate the spider. Spiders gather up and swallow their webs and move on to make another web elsewhere. To write poetry is to let the object catch in the spiderweb of language.

108.

Let the object speak, not you. Otherwise, you'll end up with a facsimile of your thoughts and feelings. Which is completely unnecessary. Things inside the head shouldn't have to be dragged out into the open.

109.

Setting up a birdhouse attracts birds to come and live in it. Like so, poetry writing lets life absorb into yourself.

110.

Truth, goodness, and beauty exist in a symmetrical structure within the object. Observe Hongyemun Gate. It has no supporting structure and simply exists in a structure of itself. Once the structure of an object is discovered, there is no need for any other rhetoric or embellishment. There isn't much else that needs to be done.

III.

To write only of oneself leads to exaggeration and the words never gain strength. Writing about other people well enough will allow your words to contain all of your own stories. Poetry is to speak of oneself by speaking of others.

II2.

There isn't a single thing in the world that isn't a story about people. Because the very thing that does the seeing, listening, and speaking is people. When seeing something, try to see your object's shabbiness and futility. Because you yourself are shabby and futile.

II3.

Animals being unable to lie straight when sleeping is a metaphor for life's suffering. When I smell the stench of dog urine, it saddens me. Because it smells just like human urine. There is nothing that does not return to the suffering of people.

114.

Dogs menstruating, or snoring as they sleep, it breaks my heart. There lies my mother, my children, and myself. How impossible it is to not speak of such things! Our sadness is proof that we cannot forget these things and have not forgotten them.

115.

The sexual mores of animals put human fetishes to shame. One insect injects its sperm into the testes of another male to spread its genetic material. The male bedbug uses its lance-like penis to pierce the female's body wherever, and the spot where it pierces becomes the ova. Poets, who wound their objects and inject their lives into the cut, are very serious fetishists.

116.

They say whoever wanders in their dreams is one who has been reincarnated. Dreams are more realistic than reality, and reality is dreams in more intense form. Poetry is the short dream dreamed between realities, which are also dreams.

117.

Put a handle on the object you are trying to write into a poem. There's no need to worry about where to put it. A poem's handle can be put anywhere your reach extends.

118.

That which we think of ourselves is simply vanity. The things we throw out, that's where our true selves lie. Things we throw out because we don't want to look at them, or because we don't know how important they are. Always cherish what's neglected and abandoned. Literature is that which saves the things that have been abandoned by the world.

119.

The most useless things are the most useful. To realize this, continuous practice is required. Behold the soccer player in training. They can turn around completely at the blow of a whistle.

120.

A true player can read the other players' hands. When

writing poetry, don't gather "gwang" but "pi". Love isn't something faraway. Treasure is in all the things thrown out by others.

121.

When writing, try writing down stray thoughts. The stray thoughts of life are the stuff of truths in poetry, and the truths of life are merely stray thoughts in poems. The things that contain the most of ourselves are in the very things we throw out as useless.

122.

Stray thoughts are the thoughts most like the person having them, and they are the true essence of life. With-in them are dreams, love, desire, hope, everything. Once in contact with the channel for stray thoughts, there is no more me, or you, or stray thought itself.

123.

They say the first rays created at the birth of the universe are caught as noise late at night on television after the broadcasts end. And that the sound of an ambulance growing farther and farther away inspired the discovery that space is expanding. Don't ignore the stray noises of daily life. There's poetry in all of them.

124.

Just as we visit the graves of our ancestors, elephants travel long distances to stroke the skulls of their ancestors with their trunks. Little elephants, afraid of the skulls, run behind their mothers and hide. Don't forget that behind what we see and hear, the most primordial secrets hide.

125.

Whatever it may be, take a good look at it. The trace of dried saliva on the edge of a mouth, the greasy stain on a kitchen ventilator fan, the drop of urine by a toilet... Poets return meaning to everything that has lost it, they are doing the work that has been neglected by the gods.

126.

There's nothing, really, that one could add to special things. Always draw the ordinary into the realm of the extraordinary. Everyone is born and dies in ordinary ways. What other facts than these can be truly extraordinary?

127.

Don't go looking around for amazing things, but look long and hard at the ordinary. Like feet soaked in water for a long time can easily be scrubbed clean of dead epidermis. A good writer can show how the ordinary is as astonishing as a Guinness record.

128.

Just as buttons can be inserted into their correct button-holes, each object has a hole where the poem can be inserted.

129.

Nothing in the world is completely meaningless. To all the crazy things, poetry is that which finds the one reason behind their inability to be sane.

130.

There's that story about the sun and the wind betting on how to take the clothes off a man. If prose is the method in which the wind whips off the clothes, poetry is the sun's method. Because poetry uses indirect methods like levers and pulleys, it can exert a greater strength.

131.

Dropping a chrysanthemum tea ball into hot water makes the chrysanthemum bud bloom. It's the same as doing art in daily life.

132.

What art does is to use a special detail to restore the whole. Or to show how an ordinary detail can become a special detail.

133.

Poetry is the restoration of the whole through details. Think of it as making a sketch of a face only briefly seen. Just as one puts together a shattered skull or an earthenware pot, poetry is the creation of the pieces that go in the spots where the original pieces are missing.

134.

Writing should go from details to scale, from the pitiful to the mighty. Going the opposite direction is to risk falling into speeches or declarations.

135.

Don't go looking for what's cool, intellectual, or profound. Poetry is what goes from the superficial and meaningless to the opposite direction. Nothing is crueler than everyday life. They say that stripping a prisoner naked and tying them down to a bamboo patch makes them die slowly of piercing wounds from the everyday growth of bamboo sprouts.

136.

Don't try to draw the entire object but try to capture just the important aspects. Think of it as trying to quickly show something faraway by zooming in on it with a powerful lens.

137.

Think of a poem's speaker as a burglar that's entered a dark room. The things that catch their eye are all the clues of the objects they're trying to express.

138.

They say that if one's wife is pretty, the very ridge of one's in-laws' roof is pretty as well. Don't talk about the wife, talk only of this ridge on the roof. Those who are good at entertaining treat their guest's assistant and driver better than their guest. Poetry treats with kindness the powerless and the pitiful.

139.

Poetry isn't like a clean snowman but the bit of water left behind by melting snow. Poetry more than the joy of meeting cherishes the darkness of yearning. What else can poetry speak of but of the yet unspoken, of what is long yearned for, or of what has already melted away?

140.

The most mundane things are destiny. Stacking up enough

ordinary images creates a natural flow of theme from within them. Never forget that hidden in the spiral is a line.

141.

Write poetry as if taking a quick snapshot. Passport photos are serious and stiff, they don't inspire feelings at all. It would be like trying to storm a castle through the fortified front gate.

142.

What kind of intimacy could you possibly expect from your lover's passport photo? A snapshot contains the whole life of a person in that moment, but a passport photo is just a mask that's going to be discarded as soon as convenient.

143.

The back of someone shows more than their front. The front can be disguised, but the back never lies. A poem that captures the back of its object must approach quietly, but cast a long shadow.

144.

There are more expressions in the hands than the face.
No matter how much a face lies, the hands speak the truth.
This is why the Ancient Greeks wore masks when they
acted their tragedies on stage. Doing so imbues their
hands, their feet, their shoulders, and their hips with
sorrow. A far cry from actors who do all their acting
through their faces.

145.

Whatever the object, the point where it is most comfortably
captured must be discovered. You have to find the door
handle, you can't just grab at any old part of the door to
open it.

146.

Unlike army soldiers, navy sailors grow their hair a little
longer. It's easier that way to grab onto when pulling them
out of the water. That's what details are like. The things
that decide life or death have always been the smallest
things.

147.

It's can be a huge disaster if your jacket gets caught in the subway doors. It's the same with details. A detail is insignificant in itself, but in context it can bring the whole into danger. Any writing that has no details is like a threadbare pair of trousers.

148.

There's that famous story that they caught Osama bin Laden by following his assistant. The essence of certain things do not reveal themselves as they are. In writing, one can reveal the essence by tapping at the edges of things.

149.

Some people's lives are very eventful. But if their stories are not as interesting as expected, that's because they lack detail. Leaving out episodes is to leave out all of life. Don't use obvious allegories that lack detail. Your story will split in two.

150.

Just as there's no kal (knife) in kalguksu (sliced noodles), poetry doesn't exist in places one thinks there will be poetry. Jumping into a business where there are already a lot of people selling the same thing is a likely path to bankruptcy. One has to be like the green frog in the fairy tale that does exactly the opposite of what his mother tells him: always go the opposite direction. That's where hope lies.

151.

Don't get distracted by what fascinates, question the obvious instead. Write about things you'd never even bothered considering the importance of. The question itself is the answer. There is no meaning that exists, only the process in which we make meaning.

152.

We deal with not the object itself but with conceptualizations of the object. Poetry warps and distorts language, rescuing objects from their conceptualizations. But the moment they are rescued, the object becomes another conceptualization.

153.

Poetry is the restlessness before realization. The things that excite us are what we do not know, things we accept but cannot interpret. Things that cannot be passed even between parent and child, wife and husband. Think about why, when given the praise we've craved, we burst into tears.

154.

It's difficult to say what wind is, but we can show it. Details are like that. Details are the best instruments to convey feelings. A detail can take the place of so many words. For example, what would you call a five-year-old boy on the day of his father's funeral as he plays by the funeral feast, blowing out candles?

156.

The outer shell of poetry is stray thoughts and silly jokes. The core is the faint melancholy that emanates from them. Poems touch the vulnerable point of what's familiar or shoddy, which has the effect of making anyone freeze in place.

157.

Just like a hyena clamping onto the neck of a gazelle and not letting go, the vulnerable point must be sought and captured. That's the poem's most decisive line. One must give one's all for that one line. Like a hyena that hasn't eaten for a long time ...

158.

The ways of expressing an object include turning, reflection, movement, expansion, and shrinkage. Turning includes self-turning (rotation) and other-centered turning (revolution), reflection is like reflecting in a mirror or through origami, movement is changing the object's space and seeing if the object also changes (symmetry), expansion is expanding something to reveal hidden details (microscope), shrinking is to reveal the scale of an object (telescope).

159.

No matter how unrealistic an object is, a background that is unrealistic enough will make the object realistic.

160.

They say that in order to see shooting stars, one must go where there is no light. And also, they're more visible from higher up. And the eyes must be slightly unfocused as if looking at one of those Magic Eye posters. It's the same when writing poetry.

161.

Don't try to compete with photographs or video when writing poetry. Poetry is liberated when representation is given up on. Victory is decided in the twists of the words and the details in the descriptions.

162.

They say when throwing a dead body in a river, it has to be tied to bulky rocks. That's the feeling to take with you. Any interest, sympathy, or curiosity towards the object must have that bulky feeling.

163.

It's not about meaning but care. It's the same care as when a daughter who is moving away for marriage says to her father, "Don't worry, I shall be happy." The only thing I need to do when writing a poem is to care for the object of my poetry as much as possible.

164.

Writing is like going to the well to fill a jar and carrying it home on one's head. One makes great effort to reach the house to carefully pour all of it in the big water jar; what use would it be to spill it hither and thither?

165.

When writing poetry, think deeper than normally. Like the dragonfly—when it lays eggs, it immerses its tail completely in the water.

166.

They say one knows a handful people with whom one still shares a feeling of intimacy with even after a long time. An object one has written about is the same way. The object may not be remembered, but how could one's own traces of this object be forgotten?

167.

In order to move iron dust on a laminated sheet, one has to use a magnet under the sheet. Little light bulbs cannot light up without connecting the wires properly to the ends of little batteries. Always speak attached properly to your own body, be firmly connected. Poems can light up one moment and go out the other.

168.

Stick closer to one's own body when writing. Like when dragging along a broken bicycle or moving a heavy jar of kimchi—holding such things loosely or at a distance will drain you of your strength.

169.

When writing, try to feel the tensile strength of a ssireum wrestler's satba high band. The words may be gentle, but there has to be something kicking itself into the heart. Or the feeling of hitting the ground and resurfacing. Put your object in a place where no one can help it and yet no one can ignore its need for help.

170.

A poem is lightning, thunder, and a sudden fall of heavy rain. There must be no hesitation, it must be written immediately to have impact. Observe the crocodile as it grabs the neck of a wildebeest and sinks underwater. Don't be like, "I'm sorry, but can I hold your hand?" Just grab it. It'll become too difficult otherwise.

171.

The writing must keep trying to show. There's no point in going, "I'm depressed, don't come near me!" when the reason for writing is to discover why one is depressed and how. If showing feels like too much at the moment, then a twist in the words might do for now, for the sake of "I" and "depression" to both live.

172.

Another point. Whether one uses enjambments or not, try to be conscious of the adhesion between words and write as easily as possible. There's no need to use words beyond an eight-grade level. Talk as if you're talking to a neighbor over a picket fence. Like a grandmother talking to her grandchild as they go up the stairs: one foot for baby, one foot for me, just like that, or we'll end up tumbling down the staircase.

173.

Just because you're showing something, it doesn't mean you're showing everything. Stories, when exposed to the outside, lose their power. The same pornography is never watched twice. Blatantly revealed morality and ideology are just like that. You've got to err on the side of the subtly erotic when speaking of such things.

174.

Writing a poem is like a flower bud blooming or a balloon expanding. At first, it's difficult to predict what shape is going to emerge. Maybe poetry is like a jazz performance. The process itself is the goal, and the ending is simply the moment it stops.

175.

The table of poetry is not like a hanjeongsik fixed course with scores of banchan sides. A tang-soup restaurant that brings out too much complimentary banchan invites suspicion regarding the quality of their main soup. Just boil a simple dwenjang soup like on any other evening. Even a soup like dwenjang turns opaque with too many ingredients. Using only a few ingredients allows the proper, profound taste of dwenjang to bloom.

176.

Theater's principle of the three unities is valid when it comes to writing as well: unity of time, place, and action. The most important of these is the unity of action, with the unities of time and place mere helpers. When writing poetry, nip any meanderings from the main narrative in the bud.

177.

One must have simplicity of time, space, and incident. They have to gather in one place in order to accumulate meaning. When drawing a circle with a compass, the needle must not waver from its point. A well must be dug continuously in one place, and billiard balls must go in one place in order to score high.

178.

Write in one sprint. Once thinking begins to intervene, time and place scatter, and the flow of action is interrupted. Think when you're not writing, don't think at all when you're writing. But we always end up doing the opposite.

179.

Start nonchalantly, and end the same way, as if nothing just happened. When stories become complex, its many parts start to collide against each other. Simplicity means not making a huge fuss. A wit drunk on their talent can fall over their own words but still be unaware they have fallen.

180.

Above all, tune into the right frequency. The static will naturally melt away.

181.

When writing poetry, clearly differentiate between what's central and what's peripheral. Trying to pick up both balls at the same time will result in dropping both of them.

182.

A story that has all sorts of ancillary elements dangling from its main thread will fail 100%. Just talk as if you're remarking on something in passing, just say one thing and don't make a face. That's how rhythm and images come to life.

183.

A story is not a single bone but made up of several joints. Removing just one of them and placing it somewhere else makes the whole story a completely different one. That's how poems are made.

184.

A poem that's made of fancy descriptions is mere rhetoric. A poem must show the structure hidden inside its object. Like the symmetrical beauty of a virus under a microscope!

185.

Making a golf ball go as close to the hole as possible is called an "approach". Art is similarly the attempt to make two things that are different into one new whole. Or breaking up what was previously a whole. In other words, it is the juxtaposition of two different things in one environment.

186.

It has to be like taking a look at b when trying to look at a as carefully as possible. Staring too intently at a makes a feel shy and hide. Speaking is the same thing. To express a, the detour of b must be taken. a is very shy about anyone talking about them.

187.

The parts in a poem where it slides into another direction are fun. Don't look too intently at one object, try to discover what it connects to. Being too serious is no fun. Scolding the children too much makes them reluctant to visit Grandma again.

188.

Poetry is about $a + b = c,\ c + d = e,\ e + f = g\ldots$ it keeps building on itself. Life is like that. Parents raise a child, and the child raises grandchildren. But the poetry we write these days seem to stop at the parents' generation. Instead of trying to force out poetry, try resembling life itself, and the poems will flow.

189.

When a rocket is shot into the sky, it drops its boosters in stages of 1, 2, 3, 4 … Poems also progress this way, gaining their momentum.

190.

A poem is written like a radio antenna being extended by pulling at it: the first segment, the second, the third … It's by stages. And thus, things thought of as coincidences be-come inevitable, and the inevitable become coincidences.

191.

Poems are like transferring in public transportation. For example, in order to get here, take the bus from Jisan-dong, get on the subway at Manchon Station, and get off at Gangchang Station. Normally there are two, at most three, transfers per trip and no one transfers five or six times. Poems also need just that amount. Too many transfers mean there was never a destination to begin with.

192.

In writing, the process is more important than the result. There's a way to convey the emotion that a piece of writing provides. Leave pain as pain until the very end. Getting to the point too quickly is boring.

193.

Writing poetry is like kindling a fire. At first, smoke makes the eyes tear up and sting, but once the fire gets going, the difficulties subside. The theme of a poem is conveyed through the enflaming of imagery. Perhaps there is only this flaming of images and the theme is just something like the cozy warmth from the fire.

194.

Poetry is between the image and the message. This can be explained through the principle of the watermill. When the edges turn, the axis rotates. Or it can be compared to the way a rope is twisted. Rubbing straw between the palms creates a rope that keeps rising out perpendicularly. It is circular movement that makes linear movement possible.

195.

Writing is the process of looking for a room that is a little more human than the room we find ourselves in. Everything will be different in that other room. Even the chopsticks in the bowls there will look curved and pliant.

POETRY

196.

At the very base of a poem, there must be life. *Ah, this is life*—When one feels this, that's when it's a poem well-written. Otherwise, one has wasted their time.

197.

Poetry is the will to live one's life and to die one's death. In other words, it's the attempt to change the verbs "live" and "die" from passive to active.

198.

Poetry is a near-death experience and a practice of death. Just as there can be no expectations of death, don't expect anything from poetry. Poetry is something no one can do anything about.

199.

Poetry tells us that the moment we are most alive is when we are dying—when looking back at life while standing at the edge of the cliff, unable to move forward. Poetry is that last look we take.

200.

In my childhood, we always slaughtered a pig for feast days. Slicing the neck, we catch the crimson blood in a bucket, a gush of foamy blood dropping into the bucket with the pig's every gasp. I'd like to be able to write a poem set to that rhythm before I die.

201.

We're all doomed to fail. Poetry, by constantly reminding of this fact, is what keeps unsettling those who still try to live in comfort.

202.

Whether one writes or not, one is doomed to fail. The only thing one can do through writing is to confirm there's no consolation to be found in this world.

203.

Poems are prayers. Not a prayer begging for the gods to do something but a promise to live by their will. Poetry is a burnt offering. It's to burn a sacrifice so thoroughly that no one can eat it. Because there is nothing more to lose, poetry is where the heart can finally be safe.

204.

In the *I Ching or Book of Changes*, there's an image (水雷屯) of a lightning bolt zigzagging up from the water, symbolizing creation and the hardships of birth. The last character of this image (屯) particularly looks like a sprout growing and twisting its way out of the earth. Desperately flailing where there's no escape, surviving by all means possible. Perhaps poems are like that, too.

205.

The limits of human beings and the limits of life are the same, and these are the limits of poetry. Poetry is the exploration and search for that which we cannot live without. The denial of everything outside of that is the affirmation that poetry can give.

206.

Literature is like a clown walking a wire. A rod is the most common tool there is, but a balancing rod to that clown is a matter of life or death.

207.

Literature has to approach hunger. Hungry stories are always fresh no matter how many times they're told. This hunger not even God can put asunder.

208.

There has to be an image of shade for a feeling of depth. Even better if there's a discomfort one can't spit out or swallow. Poems are written to get at one of those images.

209.

That which cannot be translated or interpreted, and yet can't be given up on either, is poetry. That's why poems can be read again and again.

210.

Poems are painful. They wound the object and expose the naked face of it. A good poem is like the ramblings of someone deranged. It can be read over and over again and not be well-understood, but it only needs to be read once to not be forgotten.

211.

The Pope on a recent visit to Korea said, "The peace we have now was stolen from someone else." Can there ever be a more heartbreaking poem than this line? A poem is an arrow that pierces directly into our hearts and can never be pulled out.

212.

Lies and culture are comfortable, but truth is uncomfortable. Poetry writing is the illumination of truth by making oneself and others uncomfortable. Or to make oneself and others uncomfortable by illuminating the truth.

213.

Poetry delays or pauses meaning to awaken the reader from stupor. Just as there is always somewhere in our bodies where it hurts, every poem needs a point where it aches.

214.

A kind piece of writing is boring. Writing that's a little rude and sassy isn't quite without charm. More than anything else, writing has to be frosted over with murderous intent. Obviously, this murderous intent is directed at the writer themselves.

215.

Poetry is a whisper that makes readers jump out of their skin. I once had a student who said to me, "Professor, please lend me your ear," and whispered into it a curse so vile I could never repeat it. Poetry is also talking to oneself that risks one's life. Like that recent case where a woman was making love to her husband and she called out another man's name, and her husband strangled her to death.

216.

Every piece of writing needs a moment where blood circulates. We've all seen videos of a boxer being punched in the jaw in slow motion. That feeling of going concave — that's the feeling we need to give to the reader.

217.

Poetry is like acupuncture: alleviating pain by accurately piercing the affected area. No pharmaceuticals or operations, just a little prick to take away one's suffering. Like eastern medicine, poetry has a long history.

218.

If an acupuncture needle makes it to just the right spot, there's no need for physical therapy. One must write so intently that one's head would spin if hit on the chin. One must write like an Inca priest ripping out the heart of a sacrificial child. In the midst of despair, there is no feeling of despair—only disgust.

219.

Write not like freezing midwinter but like the cold of March that seeps into one's sleeves. That feeling of a dead squirrel lying on a pine needle path as if asleep, that's poetry.

220.

Poetry has to be like the low sigh of someone standing at a dead end. Or a chime of a navigation program that sounds when a problematic area is passed. Otherwise, one has taken only the easy roads that go around obstacles.

221.

If a poem is read and the reaction is, "So what," that poem is far from being complete.

222.

Freud's four aspects of "dream-work" are just like the four methods of poetry-writing: condensation, displacement, figurability, and secondary revision. Just as the sleeper's desires are fulfilled through these processes, speaking nevertheless that which cannot be spoken is the "wish fulfillment" of poetry.

223.

Stepping on a bicycle pedal when the chain is engaged and stepping on one when the chain has fallen off are two very different feelings. Just as life isn't completely comfortable, a poem should also not always be comfortable. As in love or exercise, there must be points of pain for the poem to be real.

224.

Poetry is the harsh journey from the known toward the unknown. Think of a snake's skin as it slithers across the hot desert. But even that, in time, would feel as natural as walking on one's feet.

225.

A poem is the short journey from the known to the unknown. That journey creates knowledge, and when we return from that journey, we've become a different person.

226.

If the speaker of the poem's words is too fluent, the reader doesn't trust them. Speaking well is like the chain of your bicycle falling off the spokes. Try to speak more awkwardly. Most of the poems we write aren't hardwood but particle boards with a plastic wood veneer.

227.

Poetry is like the powdery sugar that seeps out from dried persimmons. One mustn't douse the persimmon with flour just because it doesn't have the sugary residue.

228.

A teahouse decorated with plastic flowers makes the place look like a funeral parlor. Don't write poems that are like dried flowers, make lush, real flowers bloom.

229.

Why, sometimes, does a poem that has all the correct outward elements of a poem not move the heart? *There is no twist in the words. *It's so complicated, the flow is obscured. *The expressions are bulky and ungainly, like words written with an unsharpened pencil. *The handling of words is slow or inexpert. *There's a sense of having grandly dressed up in borrowed, ill-fitting clothes. *There are no details, just vagueness. *There's just obvious word-play. *It's predictable from the start. *It's hard to imagine what's going on. *There's a feeling things were forced to fit together. *It's incomprehensible why this poem was written.

230.

Poems are always "young" poems. The depth of poetry comes from discontent, and poetry moves because it comes from passion. If poetry were a talent, how could we ever hope to follow the butterfly or the peacock?

231.

Observe the arrow on the Parker ballpoint pen. One must write poems that enter easily but are difficult to pull out, like arrows.

232.

One must change one's attitude towards poetry. There's no point in trying to paint over a canvas that's already been painted. One must hide the roots of one's poems. Any tree that has its roots exposed will die.

233.

The power of testimony comes from resistance. A poem that reveals everything upon first reading is not a beautiful poem. The appeal of reading a poem is to peel it layer by layer.

234.

Poems are like clothes. You cover up to not show the world, but the more you cover, the more you see. But being completely covered up is as boring as being completely naked. Poetry must remain just about visible but not quite… Like a silver coin in deep water, just about within reach but not quite… and ultimately ungraspable. That's poetry.

235.

Poetry is to not say, in the end, what must be said or wants to be said. In a French film I watched a while ago, a murderer named Landru refused, even on the way to his execution, to confess to his attorney.

236.

A poem that shows everything is a fast poem, and it will be cast aside soon enough. A poem must be hidden. Because poems are actually naked, it is distasteful for them to be exposed to the outside world.

237.

Like in a tennis stroke, the writer must not show their chest. That's because the reader could then guess which side of the court the poem is going to go. Like grannies playing hwatu, one must not show each other one's hand. Writing must happen as surreptitiously as a hand slipping around a lover's waist.

238.

No matter how wonderful a thought, do not reveal it in a poem. Instead, let readers be prompted into having the wonderful thought on their own through reading your poem.

239.

Poetry does not speak, it hides words. Or speaks through the hiding of words. To hide sadness is sadness itself. If one were to exact revenge against sadness, the best thing is to act nonchalant when sadness comes to visit. That's poetry.

240.

A poet can only shut their mouth and show. If their mouth is forced open, they should simply spout nonsense or digress ridiculously. The moment the reader understands the poem, the poem dies.

241.

The role of art is to change the world through metaphors. But some metaphors while revealing certain meanings can obscure others at the same time. This is how art can be ephemeral but eternal at the same time.

242.

Poetry is not in the well-articulated, it's in the inarticulate. When a stone is thrown into deep water and no sound is heard, there's a feeling of helplessness. Like so, after having written, there has to be a feeling of sinking into the darkness.

243.

This is from a book titled *Piano Pieces*. The author claims that while he doesn't think he's the greatest at playing the notes, he's the best at playing the rests. A very awe-inspiring claim. If one could write poetry that gives this feeling, one can be done with these cycles of life and ascend to Nirvana like the Buddha.

244.

They say swimming isn't done with the arms but the legs. Poetry is the same. Trying to use similes, fancy stuff, deep philosophies, looking like something one is not... Of course, this is the path to take when one doesn't know what poetry is yet. But one mustn't do such things, and the attempt to not do such things is poetry.

245.

When the message comes in the front, the motivation to read on falters. Write each line as if taking a quiz. Ask a question and answer it, and allow that answer to be a question again.

246.

Writing against an outline strips away the resonance, even when the reader is given all the information. When writing a line, concentrate only on that line. If one line is true, then all the lines are true.

247.

Poetry writing is a kind of survival game. Think of the first line written as a prison and look for a way out to survive.

248.

Poetry must be written like a boxer boxed into the corner of a ring. When boxed in, use the tensile strength of the ropes to bounce back into the fight.

249.

Poetry writing is like whistling. First, you must know the place where sound happens. Don't keep editing and making it pretty, change your direction. Even in the very place you sit now, just turning your head changes the view.

250.

Here is a crooked line. Someone might make a rabbit out of it, someone a duck. This not knowing what picture would come out of a line, that's poetry. Poems are completely unpredictable.

251.

Think of the poem we wrote together in our last session. The first line was, "I don't know who's over there." The first person to go added, "taking off the blue slippers they drag-dragged here." The next person wrote, "Not even thinking to look out the door …" and the next went "How many years did it take to drag those slippers here" and the last line was "and how many years, again, to take them off." It was a good ending line, it makes the slippers tell a whole story about someone's life. This isn't some great wisdom, just something that happens on its own when one writes.

252.

The poetic comes from deviating. Neurosis isn't automatically poetry, but poems are neurotic. A poem is a coherent rambling. If there is only coherence or only rambling, poetry disappears.

253.

Poetry makes the unfamiliar familiar and the familiar unfamiliar. When writing a poem, begin at a place of unknowing. Extend one's hand to the unknown, lean on it. True poetry comes from what has never been seriously thought of as poetry.

254.

In America, they have trees that are up to 150m tall. They don't absorb water from their roots but through their leaves and stems. They drink from the fog at dawn or from clouds. Poems are like this. If there is a tree that flowers in the roots and not the stems, poetry is probably something like that.

255.

A cone looks like a dot from above, a circle from below, a triangle from the side, and when sliced at a slant, it's an oval. It is all of these shapes and yet none of them. Poetry is something like this. Poetry says the flower is a hen, or more precisely, the flower was a hen and will be a hen.

256.

Always go backward. Poetry makes the faint clear, the invisible visible, the same different, and the nonexistent exist. Instead of saying, "I'm alive", say "I'm dead". Saying "hope is despair"—the proving of it is poetry.

257.

This changing the coincidental to the inevitable in poetic imagination is no different from scientific imagination. Poetry is also a process of problem-solving and precise experimentation. But don't forget, it is also a prank and a game.

258.

The present shows us the past, concepts show us the material, the state of things shows us movement, and geometry shows us algebra. That's poetry.

259.

Poetry is the speed at which random thoughts flitter through the mind. The feeling of poetry is also that of a mélange of things. Your lover, smelling of assorted anju dishes and soju, drunkenly trying to kiss you—what else can this feeling be?

260.

What kind of love is it when one loves someone good? It's when one loves something unlovable that makes it love. Perhaps poetry is the expression of such inexpressibleness.

261.

The vague is the most precise. Why? Because life is fundamentally vague. Only when the words just about elude one's grasp can they have power. Poetry isn't exactly philosophy, but if a poem is caught philosophizing, that's just bullshit philosophy. In poetry, it's edgier to not use edgy language. Don't show off your knowledge. Fundamentally, we're all ignorant.

262.

Writing philosophically or abstractly makes poetry run away as fast as it can. Just mumble along like someone who doesn't know anything. There are no words more vivid than that of a deranged person. Say something that will make the reader pay attention. This means becoming deranged. Only then will the reader trust and follow.

263.

Trying to get someone else to understand something one doesn't understand oneself is a con. Seon poetry feels like the epitome of poetry itself, but it's really the point where poetry breaks down.

264.

Really good philosophy doesn't give an impression of being philosophy. Don't saddle your reader with too serious a story. Toss your thoughts into the ocean and keep talking about something else. The more you bury everything, the more powerful your words become.

265.

Literature is something we obtain not by making but by throwing away. After everything that is important in the world is thrown away, literature is what remains. One shall lose if one tries to gain, and gain if one tries to lose — this truism also applies to literature.

266.

They say that when scolding children, it's important to calm one's anger first. Otherwise, the children will be overwhelmed by one's anger. Also, one must not scold children if they commit too great a mistake; they already know what they did wrong. Poetry is the same. Don't put your emotions into poetry, let your emotions settle before you write.

267.

We live within a culture, but the portion culture takes up in life is very small. Just a few steps and one is up against a dead end. Culture is like a bedroom in an apartment. It could look very fancy, but ripping up the floor reveals cement. Poetry is the wilderness that culture cannot completely cover.

268.

Just as letters written with chalk remain faintly on the blackboard after they've been erased, there are traces in our memory that remain even when the memory has ' disappeared. Poetry is the process of moving these traces to the page.

269.

They call the offspring between a zebra and a donkey a "zeedonk." It looks very peculiar. Its body is of a donkey but its legs have the stripes of a zebra. Poetry is like those stripes.

270.

There are no edges in human-centricism. Culture is about erasing edges, and making edges is countercultural. One can only make edges in an empty wasteland without any knowledge or any money. Poetry is also about putting down one's weapons to fight hand-to-hand.

271.

Poetic consciousness is like switching horses in the olden days at horse stations. The opposite is sayings like this one: "A good phrase is like the stake that keeps a donkey tied down for a thousand years."

272.

Don't attach your interpretation. The moment one goes, "Well, actually ..." the reader will toss away the book.

Simply show. Don't sit the reader down in the dark and mumble, "I'm right here …" or they'll fall asleep. Don't play "twenty questions" with the reader. Three or four are enough.

273.

The weaker the person, the stronger their words are. Making a habit of words like "the most" or "the best" makes one rather neurotic. Using strong words in writing poetry is like dousing a fire that had just been carefully kindled with great effort.

274.

The Book of Changes has a line that goes, "When the king hunts, he blocks three sides but keeps one side open." In other words, he gives the hunted animal a way out. A good poem never comes to a conclusion. This never coming to a conclusion protects the life of the poem.

275.

Even after having seen the whole thing, one must take one more look to see what could not be seen. When listening

to someone else's words, one must listen for the silences
between words as well. Take one more step from the point
that looks like the very end. Even after light has faded,
there's still that feeling of fading that remains.

276.

Erase one's whole past and begin with "And". One will
find the innermost wounds, the rough things one had
never looked back at before floating up to the surface. Our
true selves are what comes after "and".

277.

The sight of scolded children sobbing in their sleep is an
image that is unforgettable. There are so many things that
had to be left behind without having been given closure.
This fall will come and go, and it may come again next
year, or never again. Even when one isn't loved or unable
to love, there's a knot that remains. Poetry is what unties,
much too late, this knot.

278.

A wounded pinkie toe, that's poetry.

279.

Everyone has seen the twisted feet of world-class ballerina Kang Sujin. Her toe shoes have mangled and mashed up her toes. When she performs, she is said to pack them with beef. That's poetry. Poetry is what must be done when nothing else can be done.

280.

Our everyday lives are endless repetitions of freezing and thawing. The tedious beauty of it! There isn't much that can be decided or controlled, all that one can do is endure. One writes poetry so that one doesn't need consolation, to become a little stronger.

281.

When peeing in the winter, one shivers a little; they say this is because the body's temperature drops a little. Reading a poem is often also accompanied by a brief shiver. Not trembling like a tree in the wind ... Poetry and urinating both produce the same reaction perhaps because they both come from repeated, everyday living.

282.

A poem is not some grand thing. It's like in a restaurant when you put your shoes back on, you turn the shoes of the person coming after you around for them. Poetry is moving from an ugly place to a slightly prettier one. If not even that, waking up from a long dream and falling asleep again.

283.

There's that story of the monk that would bathe and never use a towel after. Because he would be leaving skin cells in the world. They say the prettiest thing and the ugliest thing in the world is people. Ugly things look ugly, and pretty things look pretty. Poetry is what makes us glance one more time at what is pretty than what is ugly.

284.

In golf, the movement of the axis and the orbit are everything. Poetry as well moves the center from the self to the other and from the profane to the sacred, making the largest and most beautiful orbit.

285.

Compared to baseball, a poem's strike zone is different for every reader. Poetry is a ball that creates a fracture in reality and breaks down the idea of the strike zone itself.

286.

Poems are nothing more and nothing less than making gaps. We can breathe as much air as these gaps allow. These gaps are the truest human place.

287.

Writing is an attempt to change one's perspective of life rather than changing life itself. Sucking all of Korea into Northern Gyeongsang Province is perfectly possible through writing.

288.

Some points of caution. First, if you need footnotes, that's not poetry. A poem should not require any other information. Second, it has to be done in a single take, and if you go backwards looking for the poem's meaning, that's way too late. Third, rendering the entirety of something is the same as having rendered nothing at all. Every part you render must contain the whole.

289.

The reason a poem is moving isn't in its content but its form. Don't worry about what you'll write, just write. As long as you have a good jesa ceremony, the jesa food will be good enough to enjoy.

290.

The Silla Dynasty people of yore may have vanished but their Poseok Pavilion stone waterway remains. Like ad balloons persisting in the air despite all the eyes that have gazed upon them have moved on. As such, poetry will always remain even if we disappear. Like a skull dried out with age… even without anyone to be sad or joyful or to dream…

WRITING

291.

The speaker of a poem and the poet themselves are like a boxer in the ring and the boxer's coach standing outside the ring. The poet can't enter the frame of the poem and must give all their knowledge and will to the speaker moving in the frame.

292.

The speaker of a poem must be like a sac spider that ties itself down so its babies can eat its body.

293.

The poem's speaker is like an endoscope that enters the object of the poem instead of the poet. How else could the poet look inside the object without the speaker? The speaker is also a kind of drone or unmanned plane. It can go up to altitudes and see angles of the object the poet is unable to.

294.

When we write a letter, we experience a strange space. To the friends and spouses we use the most informal language with, we suddenly become very formal. I wonder if the poem's speaker also lives in such a space, a space that is of our daily lives and yet is separate or different from it at the same time. A space where age, gender, or the binary of life and death have either untouched or retreated from — a space only the speaker can enter.

295.

In the countryside, there's a tool called the flail that's used for threshing. It has a handle with another stick attached to one end that you can spin in the air, and this is what's used to thresh grains. What makes it tricky to handle is that one must keep thinking of its two parts as separate, and they say golf runs on a similar principle. I wonder if this tricky-to-master principle is the very principle of poetry itself. A poem is written by a poet, but the person that actually speaks it is the speaker. If we forget this, we get situations that feel like parents getting in the middle of children's fights or two janggi players who suddenly toss the board aside and grab each other's throats.

296.

You've seen ducks swimming in Suseong Pond. It looks like they're just floating there with no effort, but their little feet are moving rapidly beneath the water. Like riding those "duck boats" where all that furious pedaling only makes you move forward a little bit more. I suppose that difference between effort and appearance is the same as between the poet and the speaker.

297.

There are a hundred possibilities in one method. Don't forget that when opening a door, it's not your finger you insert into the keyhole but the key.

298.

There's no meaning in the subconscious itself. Only when we connect with the subconscious—when something is given form, in other words—do we finally realize what it is trying to say. This is why the dreams we dream when asleep or the words of a mental patient may sound poetic but don't become poetry.

299.

The subconscious needs the light of the conscious, and the conscious needs the energy of the subconscious, and what enables their mutual exchange is writing. But think of writing not as a jungle where beasts roam freely but a zoo with tamed animals.

300.

Only when writing is play and adventure can the subconscious, obsessions, and trauma enter it. If not, then all the beautiful details and cool descriptions will prove useless. It's like putting on makeup without the face first being washed.

301.

An artist is someone who sees the truth hidden in the folds of desire. Art must be kept open for the artist to find themselves in their desire.

302.

Don't try to make poetry but to allow poetry in. A river can't be made, but it could be allowed to pass through. Then the fish can be scooped up from that water. Attempting to force poems into existence is not only exhausting, the poems won't be freshly caught, either.

303.

Poems are written by being passed through you. Leave your thoughts to stretch out where they want to. The moment poetry lets you slip away from old conceptions is the moment the "you" of before vanishes. Every time you write a poem, you have to die well.

304.

When writing, think of being nestled in the bosom of the writing. Writing doesn't need anyone to make its connections, it will make connections on its own. Writing isn't done by the head, it's done by speech. Don't be scared of saying something silly while you write. If it's too out of place, you can always edit it out later.

305.

They say in golf that the ball is hit "from the inside out". This might make it seem like the ball will fly off at an angle, but only when it's "out" can the ball make a larger curve and carry more inertia in its body. Thinking only of the things that look like yours as yours will narrow your perspective. Writing must also feel like you are hitting "out", otherwise your perspective will be limited.

306.

Begin a poem with a line that doesn't look like it would ever become a poem at all. Poetry eludes our comprehension no matter how much you write it; only through writing and writing can you strike a line that makes you wonder if you really wrote it. Of course you didn't write it. The poem wrote it.

307.

Poetry isn't something you know and then write, it's what you come to know as you're writing it.

308.

"Ticklish, ticklish, prick-ish . . ." Keep mumbling nonsense like that to start. Nonsense always skews close to one's deeper self. Trying to be greedy and grab onto something tight to write will end up exhausting you. Don't try to speak every little thing but keep a bit of a gap. Loosen up the hands and relax. If you're not relaxed, it means you're not in the right position.

309.

The center of a poem is in yourself. You're entering your own bedroom, there's no need to put on makeup or fancy clothes.

310.

Nonsense in real life is truth in poetry. To write about something is to become that something's psychiatrist. Think of the object as a neurosis patient.

311.

A writer is an errand boy of language, not a ragpicker. You don't do the writing, the language does. To speak well, listen well. The moment you think you have no confidence to write anything is precisely the moment you must begin to write.

312.

Be ready to act anywhere, the moment a prompt is given. Let's start today with this one:

"Professor, there is too much sunlight in this room." I'll write a poem, too, and read it to you later.

313.

When writing a poem, do not use others as a stepping stone to tell your own story. Poetry is putting my own story down to listen to the stories of others. That's what true "good storytelling" is about. Poetry is not an invasion but an accommodation. Accommodation means to actively accept the other into oneself. Look at judo athletes. They embrace the attack of others and throw them over.

314.

When writing a line, the next line must be watched to see if it's rising well. Whatever the next line is, it's going to be about you, anyway. Writing a poem is like jumping on the back of a horse and changing its direction by pulling on its reins. That's the job of a poet, and it's a very doable job.

315.

Here's something I wrote when I utterly lost confidence in writing. *What I've written is my writing, no more, no less. Because my writing is myself. *What I cannot write now will be written in other writing and in other ways. Because everything is interconnected. (For the sake of myself and others, I have a duty to write what I have seen, heard, and felt. Because in those places and those times, there I was. *I must sit right here, in this moment, quickly writing down whatever comes to mind, without thinking about it. Because my body and memory will be together in that writing.

316.

When throwing a disc, hold onto it before turning several times and letting go only at the end. The disc must not be held onto forever, and must not be released too early. Poetry is the same. There are serious solemnists that refuse to release at the end, and dilettantes who release too early—a poet should be somewhere between them. It's important to hold on or let go whenever it's necessary, but more important than that is to develop a feeling for when to hold on or let go.

317.

Parodying a good poem helps to get a feel for writing poetry. It's like watching a soccer game. Aha, here the ball is dribbled. Aha, here it's passed. Aha, here's the corner kick, and there it's headed into the net. Getting a feel for all that will enable you to do it yourself.

318.

A poet can be sadder than the sangju (head of a funeral party). It is because they're in the periphery they can poke the center.

319.

Stories about poetry are always stories about everything else. And stories about everything else are always stories about poetry. Don't bet your all on poetry. That will only make you lose poetry and everything else as well.

320.

Note how there's hesitation before stepping onto an escalator but once you're in motion, it's nothing. Poetry writing is the same. Don't think about it too seriously but start it off like it's a joke. Using language dragged out of your mind will only exhaust the reader. Have the words that are right in front of you produce the words that come next.

321.

A poet is said to be a liar with a license, but I wonder if

they should be called immature rogues instead. They spend their entire lives chasing what's interesting and silly. Not that they go as far as eating ice-cream with doenjang or mix yoghurt into maeountang—that's just funny.

322.

Poetry is not a library but a noraebang (private karaoke room). Keep practicing until the nonsense becomes truth. Poetry is to question, to look around the center, to bother oneself. Then, suddenly, it goes off like fireworks. To have no feeling for poetry is to have no feeling for life itself.

323.

This work is all about failure despite effort, and to have no choice but to continue at it regardless. Don't try to succeed. This work is supposed to fail. Just do it. But don't try to take the easy way or take up some bullshit philosophy. That's like hiring someone to hold your jesa ancestral rites for you. Nothing of your own will be built that way.

324.

Writing should be done when something isn't quite clear. It's useless to write about something when it's already clear and known. What would be the point? Don't be scared, just start writing. Words tend to arrange themselves into an order and come to a natural conclusion. Start off lightly, as if going for a short walk.

325.

Poetry isn't written, it blooms forth from the self. Write as if your hand doesn't belong to you but to the pencil.

326.

Poetry is like dreaming or doodling. Just as there can be no completely conscious dreaming or doodling, a conscious poem is an oxymoron. Putting it in such extreme terms is to ensure the tyranny of the conscious is thwarted at all costs.

327.

In poetry, philosophy must remain hidden. Any intention to teach the reader a thing or two is very far from actual poetry. A poem is an attempt to learn, not teach something. Don't put on a serious attitude, rely on stray thoughts and nonsense mumblings. Philosophy will naturally follow.

328.

They say that art is about reaching transcendence through immersion. Everyone wants transcendence, but the reason not everyone reaches it is because they try for it deliberately. Just as thinking, 'I must not think stray thoughts' is a stray thought, hoping that 'I' will disappear is also just another form of 'I.'

329.

The time and space a person stands in is that person's self. When writing poetry, begin with metonymy and move towards metaphor. To go from metaphor to metonymy is a dead end. Poetry is like Isis who gathered the scattered remains of Osiris all night and revived him.

330.

A poet's notebook is often better than their poems. Some do say to write poetry as if writing in one's notes. Once there's an awareness that "writing" is being done, a kind of stiffness goes into the shoulders and the language becomes unnatural. The back of the pianist often reveals what their playing will sound like. Just like in golf or tennis, it's only through relaxing the shoulders the ball can really be hit hard.

331.

In the wide blue ocean, the fisherperson is at a loss as to where a net should be cast; this desperation, regret, triviality, and futility are the very colors and skills of poetry.

332.

Poetry must be written sticking close to the body. The poet must be a sacrificial lamb, must write only that which is learned through losing the body. They must be wily and cunning, and the riskier their jokes, the better.

333.

Writing poetry is to release oneself from one's own bondage. To not tie the knots in the first place, or to lie and say one has been released when one hasn't—don't do that.

334.

American football reminds me of writing poetry. Piercing the layers of resistance, advancing from line to line. Seon Buddhists like to say that every problem must have a solution. To find it, don't forget the methods of twisting, flipping, and rewinding.

335.

Leaving the cycle of life and death is referred to as "ildaesainyeon". This great and dramatic event is made possible through very insignificant and coincidental examples of "sijeolinyeon". Poetry is the same. Poetry lays many traps, but there's always an exit.

336.

Roads always have road signs: *under construction, school crossing, caution: falling rocks*... Writing should also provide signs so the reader isn't too thrown off and can follow along without difficulty.

337.

Watching a Rubik's cube get solved is like learning how to write a poem. There are six directions: front-back, left-right, and up-down. Normally we turn things in only the single direction we're used to. Giving up the other five directions.

338.

Every section needs a turn. Turns are there to be discovered, they're not something made up by the poet. Like a dragon-fly coming to rest on a leaf, the turn occurs naturally. When writing a poem, there must be no consciousness of being in the process of writing. What we must do when writing is only to not do what we're not supposed to do.

339.

Anthropomorphizing too often is childish. Avoid awkward similes. Vagueness is good, but get rid of nonsensical vagueness. Be quick in deciding what to show and not to show. More than anything else, have a sense for the risky.

340.

Writing is about getting rid of the redundant. The things that seem the most treasured, they have to be the first to go. Because usually, they stick out too much.

341.

Don't use awkward comparisons. Readers like seeing poets give their all. Writing has to be as dangerous as passing over very thin ice.

342.

It's important to push one's thoughts through to the end. The only way to know how far one can go is to go. There comes a point when control is relinquished, and calm descends. In contrast, to sense one has realized something is to have fooled oneself.

343.

Poetry is the will to bring into life, no more or no less. Being confined inside one hole or the other will bring nothing to fruition. Use the least amount of materials possible, but make sure the turns are clear. Write close to the body, but the entrance and exit must be through different doors.

344.

Once the path of poetry is known, there's no need to strain. A persimmon's stem, when the fruit ripens, snaps off on its own accord. They say to leave blisters to burst on their own as well. Deliberately popping them beforehand risks infection. A not-good poem is like that.

345.

Living, seeing, and writing are the same thing. We must become poetry-writing machines.

346.

Works of art where the artist's life is at stake, a work that's like a final arrow shot into the air, a work that sprang from a question and created its own world—such works are the final dream of any writer. And this final dream makes their lives their final work.

347.

Regard the traces of an earthworm after a rain. Traces that immediately evaporate in the sun. Think of how the earthworm must've struggled and thrashed to leave behind such traces. Poems require just as much.

348.

Literature is fundamentally about accepting a dangerous mission. Good writers know to push themselves into darkness or leap into emptiness. They try to become the darkness, the emptiness.

349.

Most poets do not submerge themselves. They only act like they're about to jump into the water. Don't be scared, jump right in. As long as there's no thought of surfacing, anyone is bound to surface.

350.

The character for "respect" can be defined as "one master, no enemies." Have one center and do not scatter oneself hither and tither. Don't go flitting about here and there, just keep a single aperture open, the one called poetry.

351.

Enter yourself as if entering a coffin.

352.

There must be pain in the self for rhythm and cadence to find liveliness. A story painful to oneself will be painful to others as well. Moss never grows over such poems, no matter how much time passes.

353.

Thomas Edison experimented with countless materials to find the right filament for his lightbulb, including hair from his leg and Japanese bamboo. This is like going to America and trying to look up a friend without their address at hand. Has there ever been, even once, a poem written with such dedication?

354.

Watching a dragonfly copulate in the air is fascinating. They say dragonflies are never more in danger than in the middle of this act. There's no wherewithal to take care of themselves. This completely defenseless state is necessary when trying to enter someone else, but I wonder if we enter it all too easily when writing poetry.

355.

When magpies build their nests, they fill the gaps in their thatching with mud. Some bees build two layers of hives: a hive within a hive. Compared to that, the houses we build for poems are so flimsy. It's because our lives aren't at stake.

356.

Think of what balconies would be like without railings. Only the railing keeps us from certain death. Writing is to get rid of this railing.

357.

Every word, no matter how casual-seeming, must be uttered as if a whole life depends on it. There's the story of that person who fell overboard and survived by clutching at the barnacles on the ship's hull. Think of what their fingernails must've looked like afterwards.

358.

Poetry is the daily offering up of oneself through self-immolation (sosingongyang). Each poem must contain the life-size Buddha (deungsinbul) of that day.

359.

Quince needs to be wiped regularly to prevent rot. Writing is also about cleaning oneself every day. Daily writing is like writing in flowing water. Like prayer, writing's effect only occurs during the act of writing.

360.

The Avatamska Sutra states that raising the right frame of mind from the beginning enables immediate enlightenment (chobalsimsi byeonjeonggak). In effect, the first mindset is already the place for enlightenment. They do say that the Buddhist realization through much self-cultivation and practice that one has been pure all along (sigak) is the same as the most fundamental of Buddhist teachings that every person contains the unspoiled means to achieve enlightenment (bongak). There's no need to worry over how to write poetry. That place where the worrying is, that's poetry.

361.

An artist is someone who never forgives a mistake, whether one made by themselves or someone else. Without obsession and attention to detail, art cannot be called art. Cleansing the self and burning away the self is the duty and task of a poet.

362.

Because conversation requires the consideration of the other's feelings and meaning, there are many hypocrisies. Talking to oneself, however, is always true. No one lies when they talk to themselves. Poetry is what one says to oneself. Words of truth are always spoken in a low voice.

363.

In gukbap restaurants, before they add rice to the stew, they keep the dishes covered. Poets must also keep themselves covered. Consider the red coal in galbi restaurant grills. One must bring oneself to such a heated state, else end up screaming fake screams like a prostitute.

364.

How lovely it is to observe a boat in the distance approach from a far horizon. Those who never write could never experience such a feeling. It's inimitable, impossible to experience vicariously. One must not go fishing and then buy fish from a market just because nothing was biting that day.

365.

A writer is someone who transfuses their blood to the reader. But just because they can't offer blood, that doesn't mean they should get away with inviting guests to a dinner and then serving microwaved instant food.

366.

A writer's role is pregnancy and birthing. Don't write as if getting a cesarean in the olden days. Once that option was exercised, there was no choice but to exercise it again the next time.

367.

When coming to see me at home, you wouldn't simply

bow to the building's doorman and then leave without ringing my doorbell. All writing must go all the way down into the bedrock of life. Otherwise you're just saying hello at the building gate and then leaving.

368.

The superficial is more problematic than the evil. If a superficial expression comes to mind, bite your tongue. If you betray the truth now, you'll never be able to help yourself later.

369.

Speaking for the sake of speaking is nothing more than noise. Everything we say has our entire lives hanging on it. If that's not so, then stay silent instead and become a reader instead of a writer. Maybe the best way for us to help the world is to not speak or write.

370.

Just as some people talk about "the path of life," writing should be "the writing of life". If there's no life in your writing, it's nothing but trickery.

371.

DNA is collected by rubbing the inside of the mouth with a Q-tip. Like DNA, some words contain entire lives. So don't hesitate, write them all down immediately. Every single thing you write will inevitably have something to do with you. Writing is about life speaking of itself through you.

372.

Good writing isn't something you write but something life writes through you. The words may sound like throwaway sentences, but a whole life is in each one.

373.

Spend five minutes writing anything that comes to mind, right now—rest assured that whatever you write, it'll be imbued with the essence of your life. Don't try to say anything grand or fancy. Instead, keep fighting yourself. Don't be kind to yourself. The more conflicted you are with yourself, the denser and richer your writing becomes.

374.

Why does it feel bereft after a meal with a friend? It's because you're confronted once more with your own self. This is the moment poetry should come to mind. Don't avoid it, confront it head on. Then even a dog that's been following you can't bark at you. The slightly uncomfortable places are actually the most comfortable places.

375.

When writing, there should be a feeling of rolling up one's trousers and wading into cold water. Things that are resistant and uncomfortable in life are actually what's good for writing. Writing should have a certain quality of bursting into an outpouring of feeling. Such are things you were not able to digest, and such things are the real you.

376.

Our daily lives are like an opaque broth that has sliced cylinders of leek floating in it. When we disturb the broth and the eye of the flavoring fish emerges from the murkiness, our own eye sees this and is alarmed — perhaps because it has uncovered an old self it has forgotten. In the poems we write, we must draw in that eye as well.

377.

Inside the poet is an extra person. One must approach this person as if a runaway child. Inside the poem is a crying person—embrace that person.

378.

Don't put the world on your shoulders, put yourself on the world's. Without piercing yourself, you'll never pierce others. Everything you criticize about others, you contain. Forgetting this is to fool yourself. But when it gets too hard, try to remember why you started writing poetry in the first place.

379.

We write to know where we are and where we must go. Writing must always have some part where something is learned or realized. Otherwise, what's the use of wringing one's body and soul to squeeze out some writing?

380.

Writing poetry is a process of growth. Through poetry, we get to know who we are and how to live. Everything we need is inside the poems we write.

381.

Literature is trying to stick something back when it has fallen off, or break something off that's otherwise stuck— the attempt to show how different things can be the same, or the same things can be different. Who can do this work but artists? And whom can we call an artist if they don't do this work?

382.

Bacteria gets to work as soon as a person dies. They help other animals eat the body by breaking it down, apparently. I wonder if poetry does what bacteria does. It breaks down one's life so others could comprehend it easier.

383.

Poetry is when you're made to uncomfortably realize that you are your own enemy. Poetry is written to remind yourself of this truth. Lift a foot to take one more step from where you are now. The really good poems are when that uplifted foot comes down on emptiness.

384.

We write poems to not forget. How Father's eyes looked the day before he passed away... Carrying the wings of a spotted lanternfly in one's wallet is because one's own life is so fu-tile and empty. Poetry is the record of countless wounds one can't even remember anymore. They contain not one's wounds but the wounds one has inflicted as well. Careful as one is to avoid stepping on ants, one couldn't have seen all the ants inadvertently crushed under one's shoe...

385.

Poetry begins with a suspicion: "Am I doing the right thing?" It also should end with that suspicion. A diary is not a poem, but poems are guided along with the same feeling one has when writing in a diary. Your disadvantages are good things. Why? Because what's uncomfortable is what's true.

386.

There's no need to brag about how good a writer you are. Writing is talking about how there's nothing on this Earth worth bragging about.

387.

They say the probability of two planets colliding into each other is the smallest when the orbits of the two planets maintain a golden ratio. This ratio is said to be in the Fibonacci sequence, which is an absolutely fascinating mystery. I wonder if our writing poetry is the attempt to find the golden ratio between one's life and oneself.

388.

As seeds are sprinkled in the spring and covered with earth, and as sleeping children are covered with blankets, poems must also be lightly covered up when being written. That feeling of abandonment and walking away, only to slightly look behind—that's the best. As if today is the last, the very last day...

389.

When sad, speak with the feeling of a gourd that's sunk deep into water. When joyful, speak only with as much feeling as a garden turnip that's popped its head out into the world.

LIFE

390.

The trinity of truth, goodness, and beauty (jin-seon-mi) has symmetry as its basic structure. A perfect symmetry is death, and life happens when the symmetry is shattered. If so, neither truth, goodness, or beauty belong to humanity.

391.

Poetry, life, and truth are the same. None of these we could touch with our hands. Poetry, life, and truth are force majeure. Attempts to manipulate them would be a sham.

392.

Truth is a blade, a blade of grass. Words as well. To cut someone else with your words instead of yourself, those are not good words. Don't do that.

393.

Truth is not where we think it is, but right next to that. To see the truth, which is like the dark side of the moon, embark on a long journey of no return.

394.

That you're suffering means your prejudices are fighting with the truth. Truth is not something to fight but to accept. The only thing you must fight is yourself.

395.

Do not equate the position you're standing in with yourself. Someday, others will come to live in the place you're standing in. You are only a signpost. That place is truth. Truth belongs to no one.

396.

Saying "This is the truth!" is nonsense. The truth follows the lie, it accompanies it. Why? Because the flip side of a lie is truth. Truth is simply the naked face of a lie.

397.

Last night, to save an insect that flew into my room, I coaxed it into a dustbin and threw it out the window. While I did that, a moth flew inside, which I ended up swatting to death and tossed it out as well. Every good deed I've done has ended up like this.

398.

At the charcoal grilled galbi place in our neighborhood, there's a photo of a mother cow licking its calf. Being born a human, it is impossible to avoid eating other living things, but the least we can do is not mock what we kill for food. Evil is insensitivity and ignorance. Without poetry, what evil could we expose within ourselves.

399.

Beauty means to beautify, and it's making filth that's filth itself. Try to burden the world as little as possible. We can't do much, but we can let things pass by.

400.

Eating when hungry, and relieving oneself when wanting relief can be beautiful things. The precious is always hard-earned. What's easily made and easily shown is easily abandoned. Flowers that do not wilt despite neglect are fake flowers. Every time you write, you're required to die again.

401.

The beauty of poetry is not in the words themselves but in the way they are spoken. Poetry is attitude. No attitude can be completely separate from the mind. The only thing a person can truly possess in this world is a beautiful attitude.

402.

Doing whatever you want is the very opposite of beauty. The reason beauty cannot be separated from morality is because it requires sacrifice. To want to shout, "Fucking bastard!" but holding it in and being patient—to a writer, their writing makes them experience discomfort.

403.

Slamming the door as soon as a guest leaves is not good manners. Driving away as soon as a friend gets out of your car also isn't good manners. That brief period of time standing still and watching until the other person is out of sight, that is a human time. We are fundamentally selfish, but to grit your teeth in an attempt to be a little less heartless, that must be what beauty is.

404.

Even when walking with a good friend, it's hard to walk in step when your rhythms differ. Life and pain must be accepted in their rhythms and sent off in their rhythms. All learning, like surfing, is about learning rhythm.

405.

The Book of Rites by Confucius contains many completely unforgettable stories. For example, when meeting a friend on the road, do not ask them where they plan to spend the night if you do not intend to invite them to your house. Or if a host turns their head to look at the setting sun, it is time for the guest to say their goodbyes. These two examples of good manners are poetic manners as well. For poetry itself is about accepting and sending away the object of the poem.

406.

Catching a mosquito and pressing it between the fingers leaves behind just a drop of moisture. Are human beings any different? Don't go off on doing bullshit philosophy. Once you do your loving and your working, the little bit you have left over you think of other people, and that's it.

To live beautifully, believe in beauty.

407.

Anxiety happens when you pay attention to yourself, but not when you pay attention to others. When feeling anxious for no reason, note the direction of your interest. Anxiety is a sign to change direction.

408.

To people writing poetry, poetry is God. Borrowing from the words of John of the Cross, the poet must live as if they and poetry are the only things in the world. It doesn't matter if "poetry" here is replaced with "truth" or "beauty". When Monet died, he said he had seen nothing that was truly ugly in this world, and Rodin once said anything can be an object of pilgrimage.

409.

0, 1, 2, 3, 5, 8, 13, 21, 34, 55, 89, 144 ... The Fibonacci sequence, approaching the Golden Ratio, appears all over the natural world. Perhaps poetry's dream towards truth, goodness, and beauty is also an infinite approach towards this Golden Ratio. And the merit that they talk of in Buddhism, or karma, might follow the order of the Fibonacci sequence. The present me is a fruit of the years lived so far, and the seed to all the years left to live.

410.

A circle is a circle for a reason: its center holds the lines from going beyond the circumference. This is how the circle can maintain the most perfect curve and have the widest area.

411.

Writing a poem changes your life. What actually changes is the direction you're facing as you stand, not where you stand in itself. As all the points of a circle look toward the center, all the directions point to o. That's the place where you lay everything down.

412.

Just as a fisherman cannot predict what they'll catch, no one knows what will show up in their writing. Instead, try to maintain an attitude of discovering things without searching for them. Planning and predicting are only the beginning of things.

413.

The damages of excessive intent can be mitigated with the opposite of that intent. If your determination to write has ruined your poem, try thinking, 'I will never write poetry again!' The point is to force a change in perspective. Remember that whatever adversary you thought you were dealing with, the real adversary is yourself. Ignorance, resentment, and hate cannot become poetry—that's a timeless truth.

414.

In tennis, the objective is to hit the ball in front of you. If the ball is hit from behind you, a lesser amount of force is converted. Poetry also requires a conversion in thinking. An example: the child is the father of the man, and not the other way around. Try it—why not? The decisive moments that change a life comes from such minor conversions in thought.

415.

To change your life you must change your thoughts, and to change your thoughts you must change the metaphor. It's difficult to believe and I hardly agree myself, but there is no other heaven beyond writing.

416.

Only the metaphors you make yourself can be your own knowledge, and only your own knowledge can be your life. To use other people's metaphors is like renting someone else's house to live in. They say beasts rubbing their bodies on trees and leaving their scent is a way of marking their territory. And that a one-night stand can only be forgotten in the grave. That's what metaphors are like.

417.

Recall that scene in the story of the swan princes where their little sister spends all night knitting shirts from nettles and throws them toward the swans. As such, there can be no transformation without sacrifice and dedication.

418.

Poetry is the squirming of desire, the primal scream of disharmony. To see the bare flesh, one must rip off the scabs. Art is about living your life naked.

419.

If you care only about what you think, you're an eccentric. If you care only about what others think, you're a snob. The thing about snobs is they don't know they're snobs. There's a high chance that a person who thinks others are snobs is a snob themselves, but anyone who thinks they themselves are snobs are very likely not to be. The same goes for eccentrics.

420.

Rage is a reaction to when the self has been wounded. A tree that has fallen on its side in a storm can also be rage. But the reason a tree does not look like it minds is because it doesn't take it personally. I fly into a rage often. You shouldn't. Rage is evidence of weakness.

421.

When writing poetry, there needs to be a feeling of being carried by a horse. Those whose center of gravity is not in their bellybutton but their mouth will never get back up once they fall.

422.

In France, they say they swallow one's words, and in Japan, that they swallow tears. The more good is covered up and goes unmentioned, the more powerful it becomes, and the more hidden sadness is, the bigger it gets. Expressing sentiments like "sadness is inexpressible" is what literature does. Poetry isn't about unraveling the self but tightening the knots.

423.

They say poetry and romantic relationships are similar. The deeper into it you go the more you should get out of it, but when you try to get out of it, you're stuck.

424.

Go all the way past the point of no return. No one can go to the very end, but it's possible to say who got further than whom. The measure of one's humanity is decided by how far they go beyond being human.

425.

Don't be upset if someone treats you harshly without reason. Instead, assess yourself to see if there's something wrong with you. If you have no fault, it's the other person's problem, so ignore it. They say a letter that hasn't been received is returned to sender.

426.

Concentrating on someone's bad points makes the good points invisible. But looking at their good points makes their bad points visible, too. Focusing on the small things makes the big things behind them invisible. But looking at the big things makes the small things indie it apparent as well. Everything is a matter of choice. The life we live is the result of the choices we make.

427.

Predictions aren't that special. Parents make themselves apparent through their children, students their teachers, and dogs their owners. If you badmouth someone to me, it's obvious you'll badmouth me to someone else later.

428.

Observe Francis Bacon's self-portrait. A face with its chin twisted back, as if he'd been hit with a strong fist. Observe, also, the tractor tracks in the mud after a rain. Poems are like that, looking as if they were hit hard or like deep tracks. Not a single poem exists that doesn't resemble the world we live in. I could never forget the sight of a cow last winter that had escaped the cow pen in the middle of a snowstorm and stood staring out at the white fields.

429.

There's a Buddhist saying: hwagwadongsi, or that despite not attaining enlightenment in this life or the next, enlightenment in the life after that will make one realize that the lives led until that moment were the life of the Buddha. Whether you go to Seoul tomorrow or in ten years, once you're in Seoul, you're a Seoul person. The one poem you write in the last will be the salvation of all the poems you've written in your life.

430.

Why is it so difficult to see our ourselves through our eyes?

431.

Identity is created through the Other. You are not the "you" that you know. The you that you do not know, or the you saying you do not know yourself, that's the real you. But because this, too, is a you that you know, it's not the real you either. Writing is where the flipping of self and Other continuously occurs.

432.

Poetry changes depending on whether you emphasize the writer, the object, language, or the reader. Emphasizing one too much creates a deformed poem and being deficient in even one makes it an impotent one. The concept of "me" is also the same. "I am my own master" (Attahi attano natho), and "the self is the protector of self," they say. One must keep taking stock of oneself to ensure one is not deformed or impotent.

433.

The world we live in is not a world but a concept of a world. This means it can be conceptually rearranged at any time. To believe this concept is a world is like drinking one's own piss or being haunted by one's own ghost. Not that concepts should be ignored. Just as there is no nature without culture, without concepts, there's no way of rearranging the world.

434.

Teachers are the mirrors of our present selves and our present state of affairs. Just as some mirrors have lumpy surfaces or the mercury is peeling in the back or they're cloudy with dust on the surface, no teacher can be a perfect mirror. Just as Koreans say, "Believing in people leads you to hell," believing in a teacher may lead to you finding yourself in Hades.

435.

Writing and the mind need to be examined frequently else you'll end up hurting yourself and others. Unlike ethics, which is a cunning sensitivity to the reactions of others, morality is about taking responsibility for yourself. The unlimited responsibility one takes of oneself! Realizing one's passivity is the beginning of morality. A passive person is worse than being someone who does nothing.

436.

Life and writing are congruent. You must write correctly to live correctly. This is the only study one needs to do for life. The more you study the more you suffer, but if you don't study, you'll never be able to tell if your leg to stand on is yours or someone else's. To not have pretensions of greatness and to not look down on anyone, you must continue studying. The important thing, always, is not talent or ability, but attitude and direction.

437.

Writing is like discerning a three-dimensional object from its two-dimensional shadow. This is possible only in dreams. No matter how much you add or multiply, life never amounts to 100%. Realizing you will never have 100% life no matter what you do, that's writing.

438.

The things we know are so few. Thinking you actually know something is a big mistake. Stop putting on airs about what you know and don't be uncomfortable about not knowing. There's nowhere more to fall once you admit you don't know. You'll hurt yourself and others less. A poem is a warning that says, "It's only that we don't know!"

439.

They say the ability to linger in suspicion and anxiety is a "passive ability." If we can stand it, to not know isn't necessarily a bad thing. Because sometimes, a little knowledge can turn one egotistical and arrogant. The people who know to say, "I don't really know"—they're the really dangerous ones.

440.

Knowledge is the ability to withstand the state of not knowing. Try not to avoid not knowing. It's worse to speak as if you know something. If you don't know, you can always wait until you do. Waiting is hard, but it's a good thing.

441.

There's nothing that specifically needs to be known. One may worry over the meaning of life, but aside from "worrying," there's nothing much to life. It's because you set out to look for it that you lose it, that you try to escape you end up trapped. Not that you don't end up losing or getting trapped if you don't set out to search or escape. You're damned if you do and damned if you don't. Then what should you do? THEN WHAT SHOULD YOU DO.

442.

A poem is when the unspeakable is delayed to the very end. Bite your tongue and withstand it for as long as possible. What am I talking about? That this life itself is futile.

443.

There's a Buddhist term called ryukryumun." It means "to go against the flow", and it's a determination not to do what your body and mind tells you to. Perhaps writing is also a struggle against the indentured servitude to body and mind.

444.

Humans are chained to their creations. Love and death, even the self are all creations. Epicurus' words, "I've experienced many things in this life, but in truth, absolutely nothing happened," are an essential antidote.

445.

This world is made of relationships. There are no meanings created outside of relationships. In life, it is impossible to take even one step outside of relationships. Whether we substitute the word "relationships" with "metaphors", it's the same.

446.

There are so many stray hairs dropped in my office. You may think you were in there only briefly, never thinking you've left a piece of yourself behind. While you may not remember them, they, through me, remember you.

447.

Through each other, we realize each of us is actually several people, and that one persona covers several others. Also that there is no good or evil in life, only maturity and immaturity. That realization itself is maturity.

448.

They say we're the master of all that we know and the servant of all that we don't. The moment we understand something, it lets go of us. Try to see life and death as one, to see the whole in the part.

449.

Korea is said to lose in a year the equivalent of the population of the city of Gyeongju in deaths and gain that much in births. Without this flow, the world will become not a river but a reservoir. You can't get the picture of a thing by looking only at individual units. Only by having the perspective of the whole can peace be obtained.

450.

The fierce crocodile and Komodo dragon are said to cull herds, an essential role in the ecosystem. Great floods or earthquakes are also nature's terrible way of finding equilibrium. The individual's "evil" in "necessary evil" speaks of the "need" of the whole.

451.

Destiny has never come because you've asked it to come and doesn't leave because you ask it to leave. If joy comes first, send that off first, and if sadness comes first, send that off first before getting up to leave—that's the only thing you can do. And in between, your poetry gains an expression.

452.

They tell you when swinging a golf club, you shouldn't raise your head until the ball is completely out. Raising your head at the moment of hitting the ball takes away strength in the end of the club and flexibility in your movement. Like this, sadness must be sent away first, and joy must be sent away first before you get up to leave. We can't change the fate handed to us, but we can care for it until we see it off as it leaves, and then dispassionately get up ourselves. Perhaps poetry is another form of seeing off fate.

453.

Windows create a this side and a that side, but smashing the window to get to that side also destroys that side. To never be able to touch what is unbearably close, to still feel a thrill from something when thinking of it, to never give it up to simply stay where one is, that, perhaps, is what living poetically means.

454.

Visual culture, which is born of separation, is relative and tragic. Where there's separation there can be no unity— where there's no separation, unity becomes unnecessary. One must not see, but hear. Seeing is full of distortions and is highly subjective. The thought of buying a pair of shoes makes one see the whole world as shoes. Why? Because seeing makes one see what's in one's mind. They are looking into the "story" within themselves. Listening is different. There's nothing much one needs to do when listening. Seeing requires rolling the eyes, but we don't roll our cochlea when we need to listen. Listening is really difficult. The old saying goes that when one turns sixty they understand the call of heaven, an age also referred to as "isun" or "able to hear and accept the words of others". One mustn't have blocked ears when listening carefully.

One must empty oneself to listen carefully. If the ear hears one thing and not the other, who would call that a proper ear? The ear believes in equality. Thinking of artists as people who speak is a mistake. Artists are those who listen. It's between people who listen and people who are crazy where ordinary people are. Not listening means not seeing. Communication doesn't mean saying what I say, but listening to others. The best storytellers are those who are good at listening to other people's stories. Listening well can change a whole life. Listening means keeping silent. Keep-ing your mouth shut but letting many thoughts pass through your mind isn't silent. That's just invisible chatter. An anagram for "silent" is "listen." You must, must listen. Then even without decreasing your words, you naturally become more silent. Listening takes away resentment. Listening is respecting. There's competition in speaking, but when listening, you give way. Speaking results in jealousy, but listening only results in regret that there wasn't more to listen to. Speaking without listening is nothing but masturbation. To listen you must have a hole. The hole is the same now as it was a thousand years ago. The hole only has itself, no age or gender. The ugly or the clear, the proud or the humiliating, the teacher or the student—it has none of that. Those are just thoughts in the head. Holes are just there, open, they do not judge or reject. This is how conception and pregnancy of thought becomes possible. Listening is the beginning of study. As they say in Seon, the dictum "Only this!" really means "Only listen!" Writing is the same as praying, an entering into "listening mode." By listening to the object, you are searching for its invisible point of vulnerability.

455.

If 1 and 0 can stand in for life and death, dying isn't something sad at all. It's simply a return to where we used to be. Sadness is only in our heads—like negative numbers, it doesn't really exist in the natural world.

456.

They say nature has no negative numbers. For example, the idea of having –1 apples is just in our heads. If light is 1, darkness isn't –1 but 0. No matter how negative, never forget that minuses exist only in your head. Forgetting this means dying from getting bitten by a snake of one's own making.

457.

They say the side where light falls is yang and where the shadow falls is yin. In terms of strength, sunlight is yang, but in terms of purity, moonlight is yang. Yang and yin are not actual things but conceptualizations of relativity, a kind of smoke or emptiness. Life and death can't be that different. Then what is reality, the opposite of this emptiness? THEN WHAT IS REALITY, THE OPPOSITE OF THIS EMPTINESS?

458.

The light of lights is shadowless light, which is why we speak of jingwangbulhui — "the truest light doesn't shine." Why do you think people keep speaking of such things? They're afraid of death. Because the shadow of negative numbers in their minds keep trying to pop out into the real world.

459.

The truly meaningful things have no meaning. In such cases, space and time are flipped. "Before Abraham was, I am" or "the whole ocean in a single drop" are examples of such. In the deepest places, there is oddly no depth. They say when a gate is entered, the gate itself disappears.

460.

Spreading about the weakness of a person you hate is a sign that you are weak. By keeping that person's secret, you earn the right to hate them.

461.

Resentment and gratitude can never coexist. One can't resent Person A but be grateful to Person B. Resentment towards one person is resenting all people, and love for one person is love for all people.

462.

Every life is an extreme situation; we're just like magicians who, at the end, release ourselves from the ropes tied around us. That's what the Seon concept of ipgyeokchul-gyeok means—only by fully complying with form can one become free from that form. To come into a frame means to exit it. Poetry is also about leaving a frame using one's strength and talent. Without entering the frame, one can't even begin to play the game. Switching around the frame also goes against the rules of the game. The instant one makes a fated relationship, that frame naturally shatters on its own. The space between entering a frame and leaving through it is the maze. If there had been no path through, it wouldn't be called a maze to begin with. Every ladder has a final destination. When walking through the maze of writing, you might come to a point where you're stuck; that's when you should look at the details. The details serve as the hieroglyphs that foreshadow an exit.

463.

Making reductive conclusions is what weak people do. This doesn't mean you shouldn't come to one. Consider the screw-shaped barbed wire. It looks like it's running in circles, but it does move forward. They say the spiral is the most perfect line because hidden in the circular movement is the forward movement of a line.

464.

While the life of individuals is limited, the lifetime of a species is indefinite. Even as the spokes turn, the hub keeps moving forward. Even if broadleaf trees grow on the side of the mountain, pine grows on the very top. Even if it rains before a takeoff, the sun is bright and shining above the clouds. Don't try to think of these things as one; they are simply things that have always been together. Because we believe in the dialectic, we keep trying to mash them together to synthesize a new whole, but the actual objects go on being separate. Truth doesn't exist on any one side or in the middle. Or the truth exists on both sides as well as the middle. Don't believe in enlightenment. Realizing one can't believe in enlightenment is enlightenment.

465.

They say this world is a dream that a god is dreaming. Those who are awake can see the dreamer, but the dreamer can't see those who're awake. How do we know my saying this is not a dream itself? But if you must dream, try dreaming of waking up. Who knows, you might really wake up.

466.

When you just stop yourself from saying something you really want to say, you obtain a certain strength. There is no good and evil, just maturity and immaturity—a matter of self-control. The dying soil themselves because they lose control of their sphincters. Art, perhaps, is a matter of the sphincter.

467.

Can there exist, really, a moment of enlightenment? Even when you realize the problem, the body and mind will continue to move the way they always have. Don't hang your life on obtaining enlightenment. Just leave your ignorance as is and take a good look at it. "Like a lonely island out at sea, a sea so vast the island slips into the waves on stormy nights ..." (from "Wavy Lines on the Forehead of the Moon")

468.

We don't even amount to a speck of foam on all the planet's oceans. Literature is a promise that such a futile thing will know their own futility and not make any other presumptions. To be tragically shattered, but never foolishly destroyed. Even if all things are futile, there is always one thing that isn't. THAT WHICH says everything is futile! Only by studying this for a long time can one be honed to a sharp edge.

469.

When a soccer game ends in a tie, the teams go into a

penalty shootout. A player goes up to the ball and the others create a scrum to encourage them. I wonder if condemned martyrs in the age of Christian persecution were the same when they entered the gallows together. Perhaps our poetry writing is like creating a scrum for ourselves and others.

470.

There's a saying—dangranggeocheol—which means, a praying mantis stands before a wheelbarrow, guilelessly challenging it to battle. A ridiculous and pathetic situation, but perhaps poetry is the same. To hug a huge tree and try to rip it from the earth. To go all in on a fight that can only be lost, where failure is certain. Because if we can't even do that, what indeed, can we do?

LEE SEONG-BOK, often referred to as a poet's poet, was born in 1952 in Sangju, Korea. He managed to enter the prestigious Gyeonggi High School in Seoul where he was inspired to write by his Korean teacher, the poet Kim Won-ho, as well as the work of poet Kim Soo-young. After graduating from Seoul National University with a degree in French, he worked at Keimyung University in Daegu for forty years, interrupted by a stint of living in Paris where he studied the poststructuralists as well as the tenets of Seon Buddhism. He has written eight collections of poetry and numerous other books including academic and mainstream literary criticism, creative writing, and two books of essays on photography.

Anton Hur was born in Stockholm, Sweden. He won a PEN Translates award for Kang Kyeong-ae's *The Underground Village*, and his translation of Bora Chung's *Cursed Bunny* was shortlisted for the International Booker Prize. He lives in Seoul.

SUBLUNARY EDITIONS Is a small, independent press based out of Seattle, Washington, publishing in the field of contemporaneous literature; i.e. writing unbounded by era or geography. A selection of our titles can be found below. You can learn more about us at sublunaryeditions.com